Anxiety

Acquire Techniques To Enhance Anxiety, Depression, Self-Esteem, And Cultivate A More Positive Mindset, Liberate Yourself From Mental Confinement With Cognitive Behavioral Therapy

(Gain Mastery Over Your Cognitive Processes And Emotional Responses In Order To Conquer Anxiety, Depression, And Pessimistic Thinking)

NunzioPuddu

TABLE OF CONTENT

The Association Between Post-Traumatic Stress Disorder And Social Anxiety 1

Coping Strategies And Their Drawbacks 8

Five Methods To Manage The Way Our Thoughts Are Generated 14

Nourishment 41

The Unspoken Information Regarding Anxiety. 55

Encourage Nonverbal Communication With Your Child Who Has Autism 67

Exercise 14: Rescue And Search 81

Creating Future Objectives 94

Relaxation And Mindfulness 113

The Association Between Post-Traumatic Stress Disorder And Social Anxiety

There appears to be a connection between SAD and PTSD. People who have PTSD are more likely to have social anxiety, on the one hand. However, PTSD can also strike those who have SAD. The range of 14–46% is seen in research that examines the proportion of PTSD patients who also have social anxiety, albeit the results vary (McMillan et al., 2014).

Why is social anxiety more prevalent in those who have PTSD? Living with the effects of traumatic experiences can be lonely, particularly if they are connected to aggressive conduct. PTSD sufferers frequently experience feelings of shame and/or guilt as a result of their symptoms as well as the traumatic event. As a result, they might stay away from social situations and engage with others.

Things get a little more complicated when we ask, "Can people with social anxiety experience PTSD?" This is because trauma, as used in PTSD, typically connotes injury, death, and violence of any type. Because of this, the majority of experts are unsure of the relationship between "social trauma" and the onset of PTSD symptoms. Some, on the other hand, think that PTSD has less to do with the experience and more to do with how we interpret what happens to us. This explains why different people may not experience the same event similarly. Thus, you should develop the ability to believe your instincts regarding social trauma. It's likely to be the cause of your social anxiety if it's had a detrimental effect on you. This is supported by current research, which indicates that individuals with SAD may be more susceptible to developing PTSD as a result of social trauma, which is brought on by embarrassing or challenging social situations. Furthermore, rather than having different diagnoses for SAD and PTSD, some persons may even perceive them as one (Bjornsson et al., 2020).

The Cognitive Restructuring Process

The following actions can help you reorganize your negative thought patterns:

● Self-monitoring: You might begin by observing your thoughts and actions in particular circumstances. Having a notebook where you may record your feelings and ideas about various situations is a good idea. We occasionally aren't even aware of our thoughts or how they impact us. After doing this practice consistently, you'll start to see some patterns emerge. For instance, you may discover that you tend to overgeneralize circumstances. Alternatively, you may find that you only consider the bad things that can happen in a circumstance.

- Asking Socratic questions—This is how you start challenging the presumptions underlying your pessimistic ideas. Using this approach, we ask ourselves or our therapist questions repeatedly until our thoughts are either shown to be false or their distortions become evident. At this point, we can ask ourselves, "Do you have any evidence backing this thought?" "Are you speaking the truth or letting your feelings guide you?" "Have you made an effort to follow up with individuals you trust regarding the assumptions you made?" "Is it possible to support or contradict this belief?" "What could possibly go wrong if you give up on this belief?" "Is there another perspective on this?"

Seeking alternative viewpoints: Individuals suffering from anxiety are often caught in a loop that they have created for themselves. Their voice is usually the only one they hear. Even when they let other voices in, these voices just serve to confirm their self-perceptions. It's crucial to pay attention to what individuals say and begin "gathering evidence" against these voices. Ask those you can trust about your social skills when conversing with them. What about you appeals to them the most? What do they believe you can contribute to a discussion? Do they believe that your "flaws" will never let you go? You can also talk to them about something you believe went wrong and get their feedback. Listening to good and honest voices will probably make you more aware of the errors in your thought processes.

● Reframing emotions: Once our negative ideas and feelings have been recognized, we must seek new ways to feel, think, and communicate about our experiences. Once we've determined whatever cognitive distortion is influencing us, we can reframe it to adopt a more impartial thought pattern. For instance, we may say, "Well, this event was a disaster," if we're accustomed to thinking in all-or-nothing terms. "Well, it didn't go as I would have liked it to go, but there were some good things about it," we can say after rephrasing.

Coping Strategies And Their Drawbacks

Adolescents frequently turn to coping techniques in the complex dance of anxiety management to get respite and control. But not every coping mechanism is beneficial or healthy. In order to address teen anxiety, this chapter examines popular avoidance techniques, self-medication, and the long-term effects of these methods.

Section 1: Strategies for Avoidance

It is human nature to avoid situations that seem dangerous or likely to cause worry. Avoidance may offer some respite in the near term, but it frequently makes anxiety worse over time.

Social Avoidance: Adolescents suffering from social anxiety may steer clear of social interactions, which can result in loneliness and the loss of chances for development and communication.

Avoidance of academics: Anxiety related to homework can cause avoidance and procrastination, worsening academic performance and raising stress levels.

Avoidance of Triggers: Adolescents may try to avoid places or circumstances that make them feel anxious, restricting their experiences and even worsening their anxieties.

It's critical to identify avoidance as a coping strategy since it can exacerbate anxiety and make it more difficult for teenagers to face and effectively manage their anxieties.

Section 2: Homeopathic Medicine

Worried teenagers sometimes use self-medication as a numbing or escape mechanism. This can take many different forms, such as substance misuse and unsafe conduct.

Substance Abuse: People who self-medicate their anxiety symptoms may turn to drugs, alcohol, and even prescription prescriptions. Although they could offer a brief respite, they frequently result in addiction and damage to mental health.

Unhealthy Coping Strategies: Anxious Teens may resort to harmful coping strategies, including self-harm, careless driving, or unsafe sexual conduct. There may be serious emotional and bodily repercussions to these actions.

Emotional Eating: Some teenagers may use food as a comfort, which can result in unhealthy eating habits and possibly health problems related to weight.

It's important to realize the risks associated with self-medication since, over time, it can worsen anxiety and create a vicious cycle of reliance.

Section 3: The Extended Repercussions

Self-medication and avoidance tactics can come at a high cost for the temporary relief they provide. These coping techniques have the potential to have several long-term negative effects on a teen's physical and mental health over time.

Enhanced Fear: The underlying reasons for anxiety are not addressed by avoidance or self-medication. Rather, they may exacerbate anxiety disorders by reinforcing avoidance behaviors.

Academic and employment Implications: Long-term success can be hampered by persistently avoiding academic challenges limiting future educational and employment options.

Physical Health Issues: Addiction, obesity, and other medical disorders are among the physical health issues that can result from self-medication and improper coping mechanisms.

It is crucial to recognize the possible long-term effects of these coping strategies in order to emphasize the value of early intervention and assistance for anxious teens. Teens can set the stage for a better, more rewarding future by managing their anxiety healthier and getting professional support when necessary.

Five Methods To Manage The Way Our Thoughts Are Generated

Now, I want to share with you five methods for training your mind to stop thinking bad ideas and start thinking positively. I won't go into detail providing you with information that you will discover throughout this book bundle because I will analyze some of these strategies in later chapters and even other books.

Meditation and relaxation methods: Later in the bundle, I will thoroughly analyze meditation and relaxation methods. For now, though, I want to emphasize how helpful these two strategies are in "fighting" negative thoughts. Moreover, you may regulate how your thoughts go by using relaxation and meditation techniques. Though the objectives and approaches of these two approaches differ, they both essentially lead to the same outcome—the ability to quit overthinking!

Exercise: Exercise is a great way to manage the way our thoughts come to us. First, when we exercise and play sports, our bodies—or, more accurately, our brains—release endorphins, which are "happiness hormones." This is why, often, when you feel good and content throughout your body, your brain has just released endorphins! Exercise also forces you to focus intently on the movement you are doing, which helps you avoid being distracted. Among these diversionaries are bothersome negative thoughts! The more intricate the activities you complete, the fewer negative notions your mind will start to accept. This also applies to tasks that require greater cognitive and rational complexity, but the latter typically cause more anxiety. Conversely, physical activity is a true ally in the fight against stress. Increasing your daily exercise routine is one of the best things you can do to help yourself learn to stop overthinking!

Visualization is a technique that uses uplifting, calming, and happy imagery to assist in managing the flow of thoughts. Note that I'm not talking about actual pictures here! I am referring to "mental images" that are constantly accessible to your thoughts. For example, you could begin to visualize peaceful, calming scenes like beaches, forests, meadows, and rivers when you feel your thoughts are taking over. You'll feel good about these mental images, and you'll be able to better control the flow of your thoughts by concentrating on the specifics and nuances.

Self-affirmation: This method is founded on a very basic idea. I'm talking about repeating a motion or sentence that has the power to inspire you. In the sixth book in this bundle, I go into great depth about the advantages of repeating words, gestures, and actions for our brains. For now, I would like to inform you that self-affirmation involves concentrating, during times of great stress, on uplifting and motivating sayings that we have committed to memory during periods of stability. For instance, when faced with challenging work that deters us, we may find ourselves thinking and saying, "I am up to my task" over and over. Like visualization, we are compelled to direct our thoughts into a more focused and orderly flow when we concentrate on a very little aspect or element. This is quite helpful in controlling thoughts and stopping bad thoughts in their tracks.

Writing: Writing has the potential to be a true cure-all for controlling mind flow.

Note that I am not referring to all forms of writing. Writing can be extremely stressful, especially if it's done to fulfill an assignment or task requirements. On the other hand, writing for yourself has several advantages. Writing in a journal, for instance, compels your mind to concentrate on specific, organized details. This is a huge aid in managing the stream of ideas. In the next book, the third in the bundle, I will tell you about psychological therapy that heavily relies on writing. It's no coincidence that a well-liked form of therapy meant to lift people's spirits strongly encourages writing!

Once more, the time has come to wrap up the book. You can now turn the page to get my last thoughts on the book you have read thus far.

Offer Your Help to Improve Mental Health

W

When anxiety makes you feel down on yourself, volunteering can help you get back up and see things differently. It fills your heart and diverts your attention from concern to devote your time and attention to causes and those in need.

Select a cause that aligns with your moral principles; some examples include helping children, the elderly, animals, the environment, the arts, or social justice issues. Look through volunteer match databases to find opportunities in your area. Nonprofits, religious institutions, and libraries all require volunteers.

To prevent overcommitting:

Start modestly.

Give sporadic assistance, such as distributing race medals or working at a soup kitchen, as an alternative to immediately accepting a regular weekly duty.

Before stepping it up, see how the experience fits in.

Seek social volunteer opportunities to meet new, kind people who share your values. Bring friends or family to keep you company. Engaging with the individuals you assist is immensely fulfilling.

After volunteering, give yourself some time to consider the fresh perspective and self-reminder of your good fortune. Take notes or keep a notebook on the moving lessons you learn and the inspirational people you encounter.

Small acts of kindness, such as making cookies for homeless shelters around the holidays or writing encouraging cards to hospital patients, might elevate your mood through micro-volunteering.

Let's now look more closely at the advantages volunteering has for mental health:

• Offers a feeling of accomplishment and fulfillment from changing things.

• Social contact lowers feelings of loneliness and raises oxytocin.

- Building houses or gardening are physical hobbies that lower stress hormones.
- Encourages physical activity and improves mood and fitness.
- Gratitude is fostered by meeting new individuals and picking up new abilities.
- Turns your attention from your worries to those of others.
- Provide a good example for your children and neighborhood.
- Uses routine and social interaction to productively pass the time during downtime.
- Facilitates networking opportunities that may result in professional relationships.

- Based on the function, may offer professional experience.
- May be an immersive long-term commitment or a lighthearted episodic one.
- Finding the ideal fit is made simple by local volunteer databases.
- Provides an opportunity to volunteer for relevant causes in memory of loved ones.
- Offers outlets for compassion and diversion during bereavement.

Volunteering allows you to use your time, talents, and energy to positively impact others while also improving your mental health, regardless of the size of your contribution.

Embrace Routine with Comfort

T

When anxiety starts to emotionally throw you off balance, the discipline and predictability of a regular daily schedule might give you a helping hand. Calming rituals to finish your day signal your body to wind down and get your mind ready for sleep.

To stabilize your circadian rhythm, start by establishing a regular sleep and wake time, especially on the weekends. Establish positive morning rituals involving writing, exercise, meditation, a hearty breakfast, and some outside time. Try to keep your job and commitments on the same schedule every day. Set aside specific hours for social engagements, errands, meals, and chores. Establishing a framework guarantees that tasks are completed without rushing at the last minute.

Engage in soothing activities like reading, knitting, yoga, or bathing. You can prevent burnout by safeguarding your downtime and making self-care a priority. Your neurological system receives a daily signal to relax from the same activities.

To ensure a seamless transition to sleep, establish a nightly wind-down routine that includes cleaning, getting ready for the next day, taking a bath, reading in bed, and avoiding digital stimulation.

Establishing this framework of reassuring habit brings order out of chaos. However, plan for spontaneity and variation to avoid becoming bored with routine. Discover the recipe that best suits your requirements.

Let's get more specific about creating routines that reduce anxiety now:

Ideas for a Morning Routine:

- Adhere to a regular wake-up and bedtime schedule.
- As soon as you wake up, hydrate with water.
- To revitalize your body, stretch or do yoga.
- To decompress, try journaling or meditation.
- Have a filling, high-protein breakfast.
- Take a little stroll outside.
- Play upbeat music

• Go over your daily objectives and timetable.

Ideas for an Evening Routine:

• Lower the lights to signal your body that it's time to relax.

• Store electronics one to two hours before going to bed.

• Have a warm shower or bath.

• Keep a gratitude notebook or journal.

• To help you forget about your troubles, read fiction.

• Make time to connect with your family or partner.

• Jot down ideas to help you relax.

• Do some light stretching or deep breathing exercises.

• Get ready for the following day's attire, meals, etc.

Rituals bring comfort because they are predictable. Continue adjusting your schedule until you discover the ideal sequence of activities to help you go to sleep by relieving tension in your body and mind.

Frequent Questions about Ha Breathing

To help you integrate Ha breathing into your daily life and understand what it can and cannot achieve, here are some answers to frequently asked questions regarding the technique. You'll benefit the most from it if you do this.

Q. Can I get go of my limiting beliefs and bad emotions with Ha breathing?

A. It's much simpler to break free from our current mental patterns when we use Ha breathing to enter the calm of the parasympathetic nervous system. As a result, we become more open to accepting diverse viewpoints and finding fresh insights into our lives' people, things, and patterns.

Is it inevitable that Ha's breathing will help release limiting thoughts and unpleasant emotions? Although not completely impossible, making such a claim outright would be a stretch. You might say the same thing about meditation. While neither technique is intended to release limiting beliefs or bad emotions, it is a great starting point for other techniques, such as Mental and Emotional Release®, which are successful in helping us develop a more positive emotional constitution and belief system.

Still, there are a plethora of benefits that come with meditation and breathwork. They remind me of nervous system hygiene. Why not practice Ha breathing or meditation daily to strengthen our nervous systems?

Q. Are there any unfavorable side effects of Ha breathing?

A. Since ha breathing does not emphasize rapid or breath-holding breathing, which can be problematic for those with high blood pressure, it is considered safe for healthy individuals. Similarly, Ha does not blow hard, which may not be ideal for those who have cardiac problems. If you have any concerns about Ha or other breathing exercises, it is advisable to speak with your doctor first.

Q. Do you suggest any specific Ha breathing variations for each given situation?

A. Indeed. My clients find variations #2 and #3 work best during a session. This is because they are closed-eye practices, and eye closure encourages improved relaxation and readiness for our work on change. When you want to reduce tension without drawing attention to yourself when you are around people, variations #1 and #4 come in helpful. This is particularly true for Variation #4 since my customers find the most discrete way to keep their mouths shut and eyes open.

Conclusion

Returning to Maryam, our friendship began with a mutual friend. I asked her to try out Ha breathing as she told me about her experience. After all, she was a yogi and meditator, so she was familiar with the Ujjayi varieties of Ha breathing.

She finally found the solution she was seeking. Because she could perform Variation #2 with her mouth open and eyes closed (for the greatest calming effect), she would do Ha breathing before and after hopping on Zoom. She would gently transition into Variation #4 with her mouth closed and eyes wide whenever she wasn't speaking during talks with investors to maintain her composure without drawing undue attention to herself.

Those old concerns about body language and room energy diminished as she incorporated these adjustments into her workday. Additionally, from what I gather, her business is doing well in terms of funding.

Evan contacted me after discovering me online when the tension became too much for him. At that point, I switched to an entirely virtual practice, much like he did. I taught Evan Ha breathing exercises before we moved into the more in-depth process of eliminating his self-defeating beliefs and self-beating that he had been doing since he was a little child. He quickly got the hang of it.

He told me at the beginning of our next session that he would no longer automatically book another Zoom call. He explained this by saying that Ha's breathing helps him have a clear head. Even then, he saw other strategies for increasing his teams' production.

Ha, breathing can truly transform everything for some people. For others, it's the perfect starting point for further in-depth transformational work. In either case, it can help you live a more independent life. Have fun.

Meditation with mindfulness

Think of mindfulness meditation as hugging your mind. Let your ideas drift by like clouds in the sky. It's like giving your mind a spa day, clearing the slate of trigger residue and enabling you to live completely in the now.

Accept these tactics, modify them to suit your path, and never forget that any advancement is a win. We're steering towards a brighter future, one trigger at a time!

Partially Interactive: T—Manage the Triggers

Keeping a trigger journal: Monitoring your stressors for a week

Are you prepared to go out on a path of introspection and trigger-taming? With the help of this interactive "Trigger Journaling" exercise, get ready to uncover the mysteries of your emotional terrain. Consider it your detective toolbox to find those hidden triggers and take control of your anxiety and despair.

Guidelines:

Set up your journal: Take a notebook or use your phone's note-taking software. This is the hub for tracking your triggers throughout the week.

Organize your pages: Make a page or section for every day of the week. To maintain the organization of your tracking, write the date on each page.

Become the observer: Throughout the day, pay close attention to the thoughts, feelings, and circumstances that make you anxious or depressed.

When you find a trigger, stop and consider it more deeply. To help you with your reflections, use the following questions:

● A. Provide a brief explanation of the trigger. What took place? Who took part? What ideas did you have?

● b. Thoughts and feelings: Write down the feelings and thoughts that erupted in response to the trigger. Were you experiencing sadness, rage, fear, or other feelings? Which self-defeating thoughts surfaced?

● C. Physical sensations: Note any bodily feelings you experienced before or after the trigger. Did your heart beat faster? Did your limbs stiffen up?

* d. Coping mechanisms: If you employ coping mechanisms, record them. Did

you find that doing something, conversing with someone, or taking deep breaths helped you control the impact of the trigger?

Regular monitoring: Carry out this procedure several times a week, paying close attention to the triggers and the information they are linked to.

Look for patterns: Examine your entries after the week. Seek out repeating triggers, themes, or patterns. Particular attention should be paid to circumstances that regularly cause depression or anxiety.

Extra advice

- Be truthful and impartial: When documenting emotions and triggers, be truthful with yourself. Feel free to occupy this territory as your own, unobserved.

Keep track of both significant and seemingly insignificant triggers. This all-encompassing method reveals a holistic comprehension.

● Maintain a healthy balance by including a daily appreciation section. To offset your negative attention and cultivate optimism, think back on your good experiences.

In this chapter, we've set out on a trip together—a journey of understanding and self-discovery. You've explored the realm of triggers, those elusive emotional currents that can influence our emotions and ideas. You've learned to identify these triggers, whether as chaotic as stress or as heartbreaking as loss, through relevant analogies. You're not alone in this; with your newfound knowledge and tactics at your disposal, you can deal with them head-on.

Nourishment

I invite you to explore the colorful world of sustenance, where each morsel can make you smile. If you picture your body and brain as this incredible, precisely operating machine, guess what happens? The fuel you select may hold the key to a happier version of yourself. "You are what you eat" is a proverb many have heard. There is some validity to that, particularly in terms of your mental health.

Your meals are like tiny culinary vacations that elevate your mood. Consider it your gastronomic travel guide to a more contented self. Savoring a nutritious meal is like treating your body and soul to a little getaway. Your body and brain work together as a dynamic couple, and your food supports this relationship. Foods can affect your emotions, stress levels, and even mental clarity.

Let's now discuss sugar. Similar to that alluring roller coaster ride, it's initially exhilarating but not fun when it crashes. Let's choose whole foods that provide us with steady energy instead of being on that roller coaster. These are the superheroes of the food world: foods that provide superior quality goodness and boost your cognitive function.

● Leafy greens and vegetables: Packed with vitamins, minerals, and antioxidants, these vibrant superfoods improve brain function and elevate mood. Broccoli, kale, and spinach are like an extension of nature saying, "Hey, let's be friends."

● Fruits: Natural sweets are the ideal way to improve your mood. Bananas, oranges, and berries add a blast of natural sweetness and a healthy dose of fiber and vitamins to keep your brain happy.

● Foods that are Omega-3: Flaxseeds, walnuts, and salmon are brain food. The sage wizards that boost your brain's abilities and improve mood are omega-3 fatty acids.

● Whole grains: Rather than using refined grains. They provide constant, long-lasting energy that stabilizes your mood like a slow-burning bonfire.

- Lean proteins: Your body's construction workers include lentils, beans, and turkey. They assist your muscles and mood by aiding in their growth and repair.

- Dark chocolate: Ah, the decadent treat that is genuinely healthful! Because dark chocolate contains ingredients that elevate mood, it's like a delight for your taste buds and a hug for your soul.

Here's the lowdown now: A little indulgence here and then won't steer your well-fed ship off course. That cookie with chocolate chips? Feel free to relish it with pride. It feels like a tiny hug for your spirit.

Recall that the food you choose to eat should nourish your body, mind, and stomach. So, let's toast to a culinary adventure that promotes your well-being and lifts our collective imagined forks.

Affirmations, Boundaries, and Emotional Release in Emotional Self-Care

Come with me as we explore the fascinating world of emotional self-care, which is about caring for your emotional garden and inner world. Think of this as a heart-to-heart discussion in which we are exchanging helpful tools to assist you in navigating the lovely and occasionally challenging terrain of your emotions.

Consider emotional self-care as your private haven, where you may respect your emotions, establish boundaries, and find solace when your feelings overwhelm you. We'll look at the powerful act of establishing boundaries, which acts as a wall to protect your emotional terrain. We'll explore the realm of emotional release when the weight of your emotions is too much, enabling you to find comfort and rejuvenation.

Verses

Strong statements, known as affirmations, can mold your ideas, affect your outlook, and improve your mental health. Think of this as a private conversation in which we both discover the power of affirmations. These chants can transform your ideas into positive allies and help you carve out a better future for your mental health. Think of affirmations as your cheerleaders, bringing positivity to your spirit. They're like tiny inspiration nuggets—well-chosen phrases that help you change your perspective and constructively focus your thoughts. Consider them subtle reminders that you can mold your world by applying a positive perspective (Page, 2022).

Affirmations encourage your mind to focus positively and develop resilience, acting as mental exercises. Like a calming mental massage, they elevate mood, lower stress levels, and increase confidence. They cultivate empowerment and self-love by combating negative self-talk.

Rewiring cognitive processes with affirmations can help break through self-doubt or negative loops. Positive affirmations help create new brain connections that change the architecture of your mind. Affirmations serve as compass points during life's storms, guiding people's perspectives toward clarity, control, and storm avoidance.

Affirmations help you become a better supportive friend to yourself by encouraging self-compassion and setting priorities. Sayings such as "I deserve love and care" affirm your deservingness. Daily affirmations become precious mantras that enrich your mental environment. These jewels promote well-being and personal development by bringing brightness and positivity into daily life.

8. Coffee

When it comes to anxiety, caffeine—the stimulant that powers our mornings and punctuates our workdays—can be a surprising offender.

It's an interesting and sometimes paradoxical interaction, where the same drug that gives a boost in energy may also fan the flames of anxiety in those who are vulnerable to it.

The central nervous system is stimulated by caffeine, which is why it affects anxiety. The body's natural 'fight or flight' hormone, adrenaline, is released when coffee is ingested. The classic signs of worry, such as jitters, increased awareness, and a racing heart, might be brought on by this spike in adrenaline.

Even little dosages of caffeine can cause or worsen anxiety in people who are predisposed to anxiety or who are especially sensitive to its effects. It seems as though there is a razor-thin boundary that separates an exhilarating rush from an overpowering wave of fear.

Moreover, caffeine can continue to have stimulating effects for hours due to its lengthy half-life.

When taken in excess, this prolonged stimulation can cause a prolonged level of alertness that may tip the scales toward restlessness and anxiety.

It's interesting to note that not everyone reacts to caffeine similarly. While some people find even modest amounts of coffee disturbing, others can take large amounts of it without experiencing substantial anxiety. Caffeine tolerance and genetics both influence how each person reacts to the drug.

The body's adaptive reaction to caffeine further muddies the association between the stimulant and anxiety. Frequent caffeine use can result in tolerance, which is the gradual waning of the effects of the same dosage. People may become more anxious due to this and increase their caffeine intake to achieve the required level of alertness.

Caffeine's role as an anxiety inducer and cause emphasizes the value of moderation and awareness. It's not a universally hated substance, but it should be used carefully, particularly for those who are anxious. Decaffeinated beverages or lowering caffeine consumption can be a wise decision for people trying to control or avoid anxiety symptoms.

Caffeine is an everyday ally in the complex interactions of daily life. However, it can be a double-edged sword for some, igniting worry while providing a thrilling energy boost. Understanding this connection can enable people to decide how much caffeine they take in and move toward striking a balance between alertness and emotional health.

9. Characteristics of Personality

The distinctive and permanent patterns of thinking, behavior, and emotion that characterize each of us are known as personality traits, and they can be important contributors to anxiety as well as its triggers. It's an exploration of the inner workings of the human psyche, where unique characteristics can occasionally lead to worry through their various manifestations.

Anxiety is linked to specific personality qualities, such as perfectionism and a predisposition to worry. Perfectionists frequently hold themselves to unreasonably high standards and anxiety can be triggered by any perceived fall short of these expectations. Similarly, persistent worriers frequently dwell on possible issues and worst-case situations, which fosters nervous thinking.

Moreover, there is a connection between social anxiety and introversion. Since they prefer to unwind alone, introverts may find social encounters taxing, occasionally leading to social anxiety. Anxiety stemming from the expectation of social interactions can be caused by social anxiety, which is a fear of being judged or scrutinized by others.

Moreover, personality characteristics might also affect how anxiety is felt. For instance, those who exhibit high degrees of neuroticism may be more vulnerable to strong emotional reactions to stimuli, which can lead to overwhelming anxiety. Conversely, anxiousness may be felt by those with high conscientiousness because they constantly strive for success and perfection.

It's critical to understand that personality traits are aspects of who we are as individuals, not necessarily good or bad. However, these characteristics can exacerbate anxiety disorders and aid in their development if they become inflexible and severe.

The relationship between anxiety and personality qualities emphasizes how crucial it is to be self-aware and self-accepting. Managing anxiety can be aided by understanding one's characteristics and how they affect feelings and ideas. Furthermore, cognitive-behavioral therapy and counseling can assist people in reframing unhealthy thought patterns and creating more effective coping mechanisms.

Our individuality is woven together by the complex interweaving of qualities and tendencies that make up our complicated personality. Although personality features might exacerbate anxiety, they can also provide valuable insights and chances for resilience and personal development. Recognizing this relationship is a call to investigate the depths of our inner selves and deal with anxiety's obstacles in a flexible and self-compassionate manner.

The Unspoken Information Regarding Anxiety.

You've probably already heard and read a great deal of technical definitions of anxiety. The sheer number of terminology used in psychology and other sciences may have puzzled you. It's also possible that you've already gone through a crisis or that a close family member is afflicted with this illness.

I want you to learn everything you can about this illness because many individuals are unaware of its causes, duration, or origins, for individuals who carry this nine-letter term with them, fear, insecurity, and stress are constants, as powerful as a fifth-grade hurricane that spins around and destroys everything inside of us.

What Is Anxiety?

Anxiety is the body's normal reaction to stress, impending danger, or difficult circumstances. It's a universal feeling that everyone goes through phases in their lives. Your body releases hormones like adrenaline in anticipation of a fight-or-flight response when you experience anxiety.

But anxiety turns into a problem when it happens too much, too often, and too much for the circumstances. This can seriously impair day-to-day functioning and quality of life.

Anxiety is a normal reaction that helps the body be ready for challenges in some circumstances. It may indicate an anxiety disorder, which frequently calls for suitable treatment, including counseling and, in certain situations, medication, to assist the sufferer in regaining emotional equilibrium.

That person who persevered in asking what was going on could have their strangled heart heard by me via an alternative and more approachable form of communication. Countless sleepless evenings wondering why you feel exhausted all day and then lose sleep when you go to bed.

Wondering what was causing the backache or the chest pain. I discovered that a lot of people could discover who they were and become aware of what was happening in their bodies and thoughts because of this kind of communication. I have some truths for you regarding anxiousness.

Staying in bed all day to avoid conflict with life is what anxiety requires. It is having a sense of self-trapped. It feels like you're breathing three times as forcefully. It's the worst-case scenario of what hasn't happened yet, seen 365 times.

Anxiety is the feeling of longing for the past and deep emotions. When you experience these emotions, you fear that they will destroy you, and despite your strongest desire to continue, you choose to give up. It is the state in which nine thoughts out of 10 are negative and involve improbable ideas. It's possessing a mind that is expert at eradicating any traces of mental wellness.

To avoid having to explain that the issue is not due to a lack of God or freshness, anxiety is the desire to be by yourself in a bedroom or a corner. However, I also want someone to hug me and reassure me that none of the things I'm worrying about will come true, that I will triumph, that I won't die, and that this isn't "."

Anxiety is when you start crying uncontrollably and end up crying for no apparent reason. It's the thirty minutes you spend in bed wondering why you can't fall asleep. It's the lump that emerges out of nowhere in the throat. It is the awareness that there is no need to think excessively, yet to still think. It's my mind spinning wildly, simultaneously picturing the past, present, and future.

Anxiety is waking up in the middle of the night wanting to cry after spending hours attempting to fall asleep. It's choosing not to take action when you have much to do. It's the sensation of having unfounded pain in your legs, chest, and head. Your eyes instinctively well up with tears when someone inquires about your well-being. It feels like your lungs are three times smaller, which makes breathing challenging.

It is not anxiety to say, "Tomorrow, I have a very important job." Anxiety attacks seem to come out of nowhere;

they hurt and cause dyspnea, much like when a vehicle clamps down on your chest. It doesn't mean, "I'm going out with that person today." Anxiety crises manifest as mental hostility that throws you off balance and causes you to wonder if anything is actually as it seems. Nevertheless, you continue to battle with all of your strength because you know that this will all end.

Sitting in solitude and experiencing anxiety is like being in a samba school of information overload. Not able to quiet her, not able to soothe her.

Anxiety was always an indication that you were too powerful for too long, not a sign of weakness or a weak spirit. It's acceptable to be sad. That doesn't make you weak. The goal of anxiety is to maintain your strength and survival since other people depend on you, even when your own needs outweigh those of others.

Anxiety is the desire, at whatever cost, for suffering to end. It's the inability to tolerate experiencing calamities over and over in your head that will probably never occur. It's the desire to stop suffering, breathing difficulties, and things that keep trying to kill you every day.

When you put off critical activities, anxiety is defined as having trouble sleeping a few nights because of anxiety and insomnia and waking up more and more helpless to break this never-ending cycle.

You may feel helpless while going through all of this, but I promise you this is not the end, and I will prove it to you in this book. I will show you how to win, and you will. To overcome all that has harmed you for so long, all you need to do is say yes to yourself and your determination.

Living for extremely small reasons is quite okay because you'd like to listen to your preferred songs again. Because if you go, your pets will miss you. It would be impossible to miss the moon because it is so exquisite. You haven't watched the upcoming season of the beloved show as you adore Christmas lights and are eager to witness the city's illumination this year. You're battling hard enough to be alive. I am proud of you if you are making it through.

Does my worry seem normal, or do I have a problem with anxiety?

You may have asked yourself multiple times whether the anxiety you're feeling is typical anxiety, which affects everyone, or if it's an anxiety disorder, which is anxiety at a higher degree. We frequently go years without truly understanding what is happening with our bodies, minds, and organisms. I occasionally got lost in the emotions I went through in my pre-adolescence and early adult years.

I never knew how to distinguish between a condition and regular anxiety since I was ignorant. Furthermore, I think that a lot of individuals may have lived—or possibly even are living—today without even being aware that it is an illness. Living in that manner is already so "normal" that it seems like the proper course of action. You cannot correctly recognize something you are unfamiliar with. I usually stress the value of therapy because of this. I will discuss this and other critical techniques in treating crises in the upcoming chapters.

As long as anxiety is maintained at healthy levels, it plays a vital role in our lives. Anxiety that is typical, for instance, shields circumstances. This can be demoralizing and immobilizing for several months. These are a few diagnostics. You avoid risky circumstances by foreseeing risks.

Encourage Nonverbal Communication With Your Child Who Has Autism

It can be a different experience to connect with an autistic child, one that doesn't always require words or physical contact. Eye contact and even light touch can all be used to communicate and build relationships. It's crucial to comprehend this nonverbal language:

1. Identify Nonverbal Indications: Watch for the nonverbal clues kids with autism use to communicate. When they exhibit needs or feelings, such as hunger, thirst, or wants, pay attention to the sounds they make, their facial expressions, and their movements.

2. Recognize Tantrums: Children with autism may use tantrums to express

annoyance when their nonverbal clues are not recognized or understood. Determine the true reason for their actions, which is frequently a means of expressing their wants or gaining attention.

3. Put enjoyment first: Remember that a child with ASD is still a kid and should have occasional happy and enjoyable times. Playtime should be incorporated into your schedule when your child is most attentive and involved. Seek out pursuits that cause your kids to laugh, grin, and come out of their shells. Enjoyment should be the main goal of these activities, not just therapy or teaching. For all children, play is an integral aspect of their education.

4. Sensory Sensitivities: Determine what causes disruptive or negative behaviors and what elicits good reactions. Recognize what your child finds delightful, peaceful, stressful, or uncomfortable. With this understanding, you can deal with obstacles, have good experiences, and avoid potentially troublesome circumstances.

You may improve your relationship with your child and provide them the understanding and support they need to flourish by embracing nonverbal communication and getting to know their needs and preferences.

Create a Customized Autism Treatment Plan as the Third Tip

With so many alternatives and conflicting advice available, choosing the best course of treatment for your autistic kid can be difficult. But it's important to realize that there isn't a single answer that works for everyone. Every person on the autism spectrum is different, having their advantages and disadvantages.

The following steps can help you build a customized treatment plan for autism:

Evaluate Your Child's Profile: Consider your child's assets and liabilities, determining which habits are most problematic and what fundamental abilities they might be missing.

2. Learning Style: Recognize your child's preferred learning method, hands-on, aural, or visual.

3. Determine Interests: Find your kids' hobbies and pastimes. Examine how their interests might be used to enhance learning and participation in their treatment plan.

Recall that your participation is essential to the treatment plan's success. Collaborate carefully with the medical staff and make sure you complete your at-home therapy. Your patience and dedication are very important in assisting your child's development. Furthermore, looking after your health is critical because doing so allows you to properly accompany your child on their journey.

A comprehensive treatment strategy for autism should include the following components:

1. Build on Interests: Modify the plan to make learning and participation more pleasurable to suit your child's interests and preferences.

2. Create a Predictable Schedule: Since autistic children frequently do best in a routine setting, establish a daily schedule that is both regulated and predictable.

3. Teach in Simple Steps: Divide tasks into doable and uncomplicated steps to promote learning and skill development.

4. Engage Through Structured Activities: To encourage learning, provide activities that actively grab your child's attention while upholding a high degree of organization.

5. Consistent Reinforcement: Give consistent feedback and use positive reinforcement to support desired behaviors.

6. Include the Parents: The treatment plan's effectiveness depends on the parents' active participation since it provides ongoing support and reinforcement of newly acquired abilities.

It's critical to be informed about the range of autism treatment choices available, including behavioral, speech-language, physical, occupational, and nutritional therapy. Even though you can investigate several strategies simultaneously, focusing on your child's most urgent requirements and severe symptoms first is best. This focused strategy may be more successful in resolving their current problems.

Therapeutic Applications

The ABC model's full value is often appreciated within the therapeutic environment, even though it provides a fundamental framework for understanding and analyzing your ideas, feelings, and behaviors. Collaborating with a professional therapist provides a directed approach to exploring your cognitive processes in greater detail, enabling you to successfully refute and challenge harmful ideas and behaviors.

The Significance of Counseling

It is more difficult to acquire a feeling of organization and skill outside of a therapeutic setting. Self-help programs are admirable, but a clinician's unbiased assessment gives your self-analysis more depth. The skilled eye of a therapist can identify deeply rooted beliefs or subtle cognitive distortions that you might miss. The ABC model is used as a conversational tool in treatment, akin to a dialogical chessboard where each move—every idea, emotion, or action—is examined, comprehended, and frequently adjusted.

Using ABC in Therapeutic Approaches

The ABC paradigm frequently combines easily with other CBT strategies in treatment. For example, Socratic inquiry, which uses probing inquiries to reveal your underlying beliefs and cognitive distortions, may be combined with ABC by your therapist. According to the ABC model, if your "Belief" is that failing at a task renders you a complete failure, a sequence of inquiries such as "Does evidence support this belief? Do any opposing examples exist? You can refute and reframe this illogical thinking by asking yourself, "What would you say to a friend who shares the same belief?"

The ABC model's inclusion in homework assignments is a potent therapeutic application. Your therapist might ask you to keep a journal where you would document ABC sequences as they occur in real time each week. You go through these records with your therapist in sessions, questioning the Beliefs and looking at the Consequences. In addition to being instructive, these projects help maintain therapeutic work outside the clinician's office.

The Argument in Favor of Therapeutic Flexibility

Therapists frequently modify the ABC approach to meet each client's particular requirements and complexity. The ABC model, for instance, might be modified to account for your elevated emotional reactions and coping strategies if you're experiencing trauma. The Consequences may become more important for persons who are depressed, with a focus on behavioral activation strategies to end the cycle of hopelessness and inaction.

Storytelling's Place in Therapy

The rich tapestry of your story can also be weaved into the ABC model through therapy. Life is not a series of discrete incidents, convictions, or outcomes. Dissecting the narratives you have told yourself throughout the years that have influenced your present worldview is a common step in the therapy process. In this sense, ABC assists with rewriting enduring life scripts and analyzing isolated occurrences.

Connecting Therapy with Daily Life

The ultimate objective is to internalize the analytical abilities you developed in treatment, making the ABC model a crucial component of your mental toolbox. Similar to how a musician doesn't stop learning new talents at music school, these cognitive abilities are carried over into the routine and unpredictability of daily life. By then, the ABC model has evolved from a therapeutic tool to a way of life and a vital foundation for resilience, self-improvement, and emotional intelligence.

The ABC model can be used to observe your cognitive processes and as a lever to bring about significant change. When incorporated appropriately into treatment, it offers an organized, flexible, and profoundly wise means to support long-lasting behavioral and emotional change.

Exercise 14: Rescue And Search

When you have to deal with depersonalization, grounding practices assist you in staying in the present. They might not be sufficient to deal with a dire emergency, though. If you experience depersonalization, there may be times when you feel helpless and afraid. A search and rescue plan, which you must prepare ahead of time, is the one action that can assist you in such circumstances more than any other.

Choose a time when you're at ease and composed, then take a seat to draft your plan. Put down on paper or your phone how depersonalization happens. Think about your feelings, ideas, and bodily experiences. As you describe the incident, try to be as specific as possible. Next, concentrate on the stimuli that cause the depersonalization to occur. Does something specific happen to you every time you feel disconnected from reality? What place are you at right now? Does anyone accompany you? Compare all the times you have had a sense of detachment from your thoughts and actions. Have you noticed any trends? If so, make a note of it.

Now that you know exactly what happens right before depersonalization occurs, note the strategies you can use to combat it. You can record all the activities that help you stay present in the moment, or you can apply the grounding strategies you learned in the prior task. If you feel comfortable doing so, you might approach your parents or friends for assistance. If they understand how you react when you lose your sense of reality and how to comfort you, they can assist you in developing your search and rescue plan. Once your strategy is prepared, don't forget to apply it whenever you sense a depersonalization episode coming on. Bring it with you at all times. Another effective strategy to maintain present-focused attention is to read and reread it.

Exercise 15: Perceptual Awareness

You've already found that depersonalization can be eased and managed by concentrating on your five senses. You get more at ease the more you use your senses. Can you envision all the things you typically do that inherently engage all five of your senses? You can sit in the middle of your bedroom and concentrate on your surroundings—how your room smells, the sounds outside your window, the feel of your feet on the floor, etc. When you stop to think about it, everything you do daily—like eating, wearing clothes, brushing your teeth, drinking water, and going to school—can help you use your five senses.

Engaging all of your senses while performing daily tasks is the "sensory awareness" practice. You can select one of the duties above or consider other options. Since you need to become used to the activity, I advise you to start with two or three activities. Next, choose whether to concentrate on one sense or use them all. For instance, you may choose to focus only on flavor when eating. Make a daily commitment to completing the practice to increase your awareness of your senses and all the little things you typically overlook.

This chapter examined the causes of our issues. We could think critically about our personalities, major life events, and ourselves through six exercises. We were able to determine the underlying causes of our issues and whether or not traumatic events from the past continue to impact us now through four exercises.

They also assisted us in realizing that not every bad thing that happens to us is harmful. The last five exercises dealt with depersonalization—what it is, how to spot it, and how to deal with it using easy strategies. We can continue our adventure now that we have everything about ourselves. We'll learn how to deal with intrusive and negative thoughts in Chapter 2.

Greetings, Readers

We thank you from the bottom of our hearts for selecting "How to Manage Stress and Anxiety: Your Comprehensive Guide to Serene Living." It means the world to you that you chose to travel with us on this adventure. We truly hope that the knowledge and techniques offered on these pages will be helpful to you in your pursuit of a life free from stress.

We would appreciate it if you would consider providing an honest review on Amazon if you found our book enlightening and helpful. In addition to being extremely helpful to us, your comments also support other readers in their quest for solutions that effectively manage stress and anxiety.

We are grateful you are a group member that promotes wellbeing and inner serenity.

Warm regards,

Holman, Christa D.

dietary habits and anxiety

Realizing the connection between your diet and mental health is like unlocking a secret door to anxiety management. The Gut-Brain Connection and Foods to Support Mental Health are two important topics of nutrition and anxiety that will be covered in this section. These simple-to-understand insights can help you make well-informed food decisions that support your mental wellbeing.

The Brain-Gut Relationship

Consider your intuition and your intellect to be close friends who communicate frequently. This discussion is influenced by the food you eat. Eating healthfully is like providing conversation starters for your pals. However, eating improperly throws off their ability to communicate.

This is how it operates: Your stomach is home to billions of microscopic organisms known as "microbes." These microorganisms are crucial to your general health and digestion. Unexpectedly, they also affect your anxiety and mood. Consuming a diet high in minerals and fiber helps to sustain these beneficial bacteria. Your brain receives positive messages from them in turn.

Consider a meal that consists of fruits, veggies, and whole grains. These foods act as fuel for the good bacteria in your stomach. Because they are thriving, your brain receives signals that help you feel happier and experience less worry.

Conversely, overindulging in sugar and processed foods might upset your gut's natural equilibrium. Your brain may receive unfavorable messages as a result, which could exacerbate anxiety.

Taking Care of Sleep Issues

Sometimes, even with good routines, sleep issues still arise. Sleep disturbances are akin to misfitting puzzle pieces. They can cause anxiety and interfere with your sleep.

Consult a healthcare provider if you think you may have a sleep condition. They can assess your symptoms and recommend therapies, prescription drugs, or lifestyle modifications.

For instance, imagine that even after a full night's sleep, you still snore loudly, have trouble breathing while you sleep, or feel exhausted during the day. These can indicate that you have sleep apnea. A sleep specialist can identify the illness and recommend therapies, such as using a continuous positive airway pressure (CPAP) machine to maintain an open airway while you sleep.

Restful evenings and less anxiety are built on healthy sleep practices. To treat suspected sleep disorders, speaking with a healthcare provider is critical when these practices are insufficient and sleep issues continue. A restful night's sleep can greatly improve your general wellbeing and act as a mental reset button.

Reducing Stress in Your Life

Fortifying your castle against life's storms is analogous to stress-proofing. It entails making deliberate decisions and developing a stress-reduction lifestyle. Here's how to live a life free of stress:

1. Establish Boundaries: Take time and energy conservation measures by learning to say no when necessary.

2. Time Management: Set work priorities and assign them when you can. Don't pack too much into your calendar.

3. Healthy Lifestyle: Keep up a regular exercise schedule, a balanced diet, and adequate sleep. These routines improve your capacity to manage stress.

4. Mindfulness: To stay in the present and lessen worry about the future, engage in mindfulness exercises.

5. Hobbies and Interests: Engage in enjoyable and soothing activities. They act as release valves for tension.

Imagine, for example, that you are balancing job, family, and personal obligations throughout a normal workweek. Setting limits by refusing to take on extra work, time management techniques, and spending an evening relaxing with your favorite pastime—like painting or gardening—are some ways to prevent stress.

Simply put, stress reduction for lifelong learning involves stress-proofing your life to reduce stress and developing resilience to overcome obstacles in life. It's similar to having a castle and a shield to protect your well-being. You can live a more stress-free and balanced life for years to come if you apply these techniques to your everyday routine.

Creating Future Objectives

Envision possessing a plan that directs you toward a future devoid of anxiety. In this section, we'll look at three important components of goal-setting in the future: Keeping a Stress-Free Lifestyle, Keeping an Eye on Things and Making Adjustments, and Celebrating

Achievements. These ideas, which are explained simply, can assist you in navigating life's journey with less stress and more fulfillment.

Sustaining an Anti-Stress Lifestyle

Keeping up a stress-free lifestyle is similar to caring for a lovely garden. Your wellbeing and wellbeing need regular care and attention, just like a garden does. This entails regularly putting the stress-reduction strategies you've learned throughout this book into practice.

Here's how to keep your lifestyle stress-free:

1. Consistent Practice: Keep up your usual mindfulness, exercise, and

relaxation practices. Maintaining consistency is essential.

2. Healthy Habits: Adhere to your regular sleeping and eating schedules. Don't allow stress to break your established routines.

3. Social Connections: Take care of your friendships and family ties. Rely on your network of support as required.

4. Time Management: To prevent getting overwhelmed, continue setting priorities and using your time wisely.

Harmonious Living: Adopting Mindful Lifestyle to Alleviate Anxiety

Anxiety can obscure our sleep, making it difficult to get peaceful, restful sleep. But worry not—mindful living is the secret to a better night's sleep and enhanced mental health. With the help of mindfulness meditation, we may quiet our brains and find comfort in the here and now. Together, let's set out on a journey to uncover the life-changing potential of mindful living and learn how it may help us overcome worry, spread joy, and achieve calm.

Here are some useful suggestions to help you incorporate mindful living into your everyday activities.

Begin by practicing mindfulness meditation: Adopting meditation as your first mindful living practice will help. As you become more comfortable, progressively extend the time each day from a few minutes at first. The basis for living consciously is laid by meditation, which develops focus and awareness.

Adopt mindfulness at all times of the day: Recall that mindfulness is not limited to meditation sessions. It is a manner of being that you can bring into all facets of your day. Throughout your daily tasks, be mindful of your thoughts, feelings, and environment by remaining in the present.

Embrace the power of your breath: As you practice mindful living, your breath becomes a reliable companion. Stop and take a deep breath every time you feel overwhelmed or anxious. Take comfort in the rhythm of your breath as you concentrate on the feeling of air entering and leaving your body.

To live a mindful existence, we should embrace the beauty of taking our time and appreciating the little pleasures in life. Pause to enjoy the small pleasures in life, such as a delicious meal, a stunning sunset, or a tender touch from a loved one.

Set aside some time every day to think about the blessings in your life, such as your wellbeing, your family's love, and the days that go by.

Make a connection with the natural world: it can cultivate mindfulness in us. Permit yourself to spend time outside, whether for a peaceful stroll in the park, a strenuous hike, or just relaxing while enjoying nature's beauty.

Make self-care a priority. Mindful living requires self-care. Take good care of your body, get enough sleep, and do things that make you happy to maintain your mental, emotional, and spiritual well-beingwellbeing.

Recall that this process necessitates patience and starts with baby steps. With patience and consistent application, mindfulness will become a natural part of your everyday routine, assisting you in leading a peaceful and harmonious existence.

Conscientious Self-Compassion

Simply put, mindful self-compassion is accepting oneself with kindness and gentleness, especially in times of vulnerability or distress. It's about responding to our feelings with the same compassion and understanding we would give a close friend and recognizing our feelings without passing judgment on ourselves. A reliable compass for women navigating the waves of worry is mindful self-compassion.

Turning inward and criticizing ourselves when fear comes knocking is far too simple. We could let ourselves slip into helplessness or weakness or be overwhelmed. This self-critical internal conversation only strengthens the grip of worry by reiterating that we lack the necessary skills to manage our emotions. However, we can break this cycle by incorporating mindful self-compassion into our daily lives.

We might speak to ourselves in a calming and supportive manner instead of criticizing our nervous thoughts. We can gently remind ourselves that anxiousness is normal and that we are always trying our hardest. The grip of anxiety starts to weaken as we show ourselves this compassion and understanding, and we discover a source of inner peace.

Like consoling words we exchange with a dear friend, positive self-talk can be a lifesaver when the waves of anxiety begin to rise. Picture yourself and that close friend sitting across from one other, enjoying tea or coffee. You become aware of your heart's uneasiness and your mind's speeding ideas. You envelop your remarks in compassion rather than criticizing yourself for these emotions.

You tell yourself softly as a comforting wind, "It's absolutely okay to feel anxious right now." "Keep in mind, you're not doing this alone. These are normal moments in a world that is always changing that you are navigating."

As you remind yourself that every stride is an expression of your best effort, anxiety seems to loosen its hold on you.

"It's good that you're here, confronting these emotions head-on. Even in these vulnerable moments, you are strong."

Recognizing Emotional Difficulties Linked to ADHD in a Partnership

Dealing with Attention-Deficit/Hyperactivity Disorder (ADHD) in a relationship brings with it a special set of mental health issues that both partners have to manage. These emotional difficulties are frequently caused by the fundamental characteristics of ADHD and how it impacts the person's emotional surroundings.

1. Emotional Intensity and Volatility: ADHD tends to enhance emotional states, increasing their intensity and

volatility. It's similar to experiencing emotions in vivid technicolor, where happiness may be exuberant, and rage can be overwhelming.

For someone with ADHD, a minor incident that might not cause others to feel strongly could trigger a powerful emotional wave.

2. Rejection Sensitivity: One prevalent mental health issue linked to ADHD is rejection sensitivity. The slightest suggestion of rejection or criticism can trigger strong emotional emotions. One of the most emotional obstacles in relationships is the fear of being misunderstood or ridiculed, frequently making people tense and anxious.

3. Impulsivity and Reactions to Emotions: ADHD can result in impulsive and unsuitable emotional reactions. The temptation to react without thinking things through or assessing the consequences can lead to misunderstandings or issues in a relationship. Emotionally hurried replies can cause a little dispute to escalate rapidly.

4. Difficulty in Emotional Articulation: People with ADHD may struggle to articulate their emotions. Emotions can have depth and complexity that are felt inwardly, but finding the correct words or actions to describe them can be difficult. It can be like trying to grab smoke. This emotional communication

issue may result in a lack of emotional understanding between partners.

5. Overwhelming and Emotional Shutdown: Mental tiredness can result from an ADHD person's constant activity and barrage of information. Emotional shutdown, a coping mechanism to shield oneself from the intensity of these emotions, maybe the outcome of this emotional overload. Stillness like this, nevertheless, can create mental space in a partnership.

Promoting Emotional Intelligence and Empathy Among Partners

To manage the emotional issues that come with ADHD in a partnership, it is critical to promote awareness and emotional understanding between partners. It's about constructing a bridge of compassion, understanding, and support to overcome choppy mental waters.

1. Education and Awareness: Gaining knowledge about ADHD and its effects on the mind is the first step. Both partners need to educate themselves on the symptoms, causes, and coping mechanisms of ADHD. Empathy is based on knowledge, which also helps partners better understand each other's emotional states.

2. Active Listening and Validation: When someone is talking about their feelings, active listening entails being present and engaged. Knowing the emotions that underlie the words is just as important

as hearing them. It's critical to validate your partner's feelings by acknowledging and embracing them, even if you don't completely understand them. It gives them confidence that their emotions are valued and acknowledged.

3. Engage in Non-Judgmental Attunement: This type of connection is knowing your partner's emotions without passing judgment or offering ideas. Even if you disagree with their sentiments or emotions, being receptive to their emotional energy is important. This practice fosters mental intimacy and trust.

4. Encourage Emotional Expression and Open Communication: Promote candid conversation about emotions within the

relationship. Open and sincere discussions about the emotional effects of ADHD can increase compassion and understanding.

5. Empathy-Sharing Activities:

Take part in exercises designed to increase comprehension. Role-playing one another's perspectives, reading and discussing books or articles regarding ADHD and relationships, or even attending support groups or therapy sessions together are a few examples. Putting oneself in each other's shoes fosters greater emotional understanding.

6. Frequent Check-Ins on Emotions:

Make mental check-ins a regular part of your routine. This can be a focused period during which both partners discuss their feelings, what's mentally challenging them, and how the relationship can help them. It facilitates communication and aids in the early detection of mental health issues.

7. Looking for Expert Advice:

A counselor with training in ADHD can provide strategies and techniques to enhance mental clarity and establish a more tranquil and sympathetic relationship.

Developing Knowledge, One Feeling at a Time

Gaining comprehension and empathy in the intricate dance of emotions in an ADHD-affected relationship is like studying the fluid movements of a ballet.

Understanding and encouraging one another mentally requires experience, patience, and a sincere desire.

The ultimate objective is to use emotional challenges as building blocks for a relationship's foundation of love and connection. When couples learn to navigate the emotional kaleidoscope together, the hues of empathy and understanding blend harmoniously to produce a vision of oneness and love.

Relaxation And Mindfulness

Both mindfulness and relaxation are great strategies for lowering stress and anxiety because of their tight relationship. Mindfulness involves attention to the here and now while conscious of your thoughts and emotions. You can attain a state of mindfulness by using relaxation techniques like progressive muscle relaxation and deep breathing.

I would suggest beginning with a basic breathing exercise if you are new to mindfulness and relaxation techniques. Pay attention to the sensation of air entering and exiting your body and the rise and fall of your chest. Any ideas that cross your mind should be noted, but try not to focus on them. Allow them to arrive and depart.

Progressive muscle relaxation is an additional method of relaxation that you can attempt. For a brief period, concentrate on your feet and tension the muscles there. Feel the relaxation and let go of the tension after that. As you proceed up your body, tense and release every muscle group.

You can attempt a lot of different mindfulness and relaxation techniques. A few like mindful eating, mindful walking, and mindful showering. A common activity that involves scanning your body from head to toe, focusing on each body region and noting any sensations or feelings that come, is called the "body scan."

Developing an optimistic outlook is a crucial component of mindfulness and relaxation practices. Begin by cultivating thankfulness. Gratitude can be as easy as listing three things you are thankful for every day. Positive affirmation practice is another method. You can tell yourself these little affirmations to help you think positively.

Visualization is another approach you might attempt if you're stressed or anxious. To do this:

Try to picture yourself in a serene setting.

Shut your eyes and picture yourself at a beach, in a forest, or somewhere else that brings you calm.

Pay attention to your breathing and try to be present while you visualize.

Relaxation and mindfulness are useful techniques for lowering tension and anxiety. You can work on gratitude, affirmations, visualization, body scans, progressive muscle relaxation, and breathing techniques. Experiment and find the method that works best for you. Just keep in mind to practice consistently and with patience.

Meditation with mindfulness

A contemplative technique called mindfulness meditation is focusing your attention on the here and now with intention and without passing judgment. Let's take a closer look at mindfulness meditation:

The history of mindful meditation

- Buddhist traditions, especially Vipassana and Zen practices, are the origins of mindfulness meditation.

- Mindfulness has been secularized and adapted in recent decades, enabling people with all backgrounds and belief systems to practice it.

Fundamental Ideas:

- Present-Moment Awareness: Focused attention to the present moment is encouraged by mindfulness meditation, which involves monitoring thoughts, feelings, and sensations without passing judgment.

- Non-Judgmental Observation: Students learn to accept whatever comes up in their bodies and brains without assigning a positive or negative value.

Advantages of Mindfulness-Based Meditation

- Stress Reduction: People who practice mindfulness meditation report feeling less stressed as a result of being better able to control how they respond to stressful events and build resilience.
- Emotional Regulation**: Encouraging awareness of emotions as they emerge and enabling people to behave intelligently rather than impulsively can enhance emotional regulation.
- Better Concentration: Consistent practice improves focus and attention,

which is advantageous in job, school, and other facets of life.

- Pain Management: By altering one's perspective on pain experiences, mindfulness can assist people in managing their pain, both acute and chronic.

- Enhanced Self-Awareness: Engaging in mindfulness helps people become more self-aware and better understand their thoughts, feelings, and behaviors.

- Better Relationships: Developing communication and empathy abilities can help to improve interpersonal relationships.

- Better Sleep: By lowering racing thoughts and encouraging relaxation, mindfulness practices can enhance the quality of your sleep.

Methods of Mindfulness Meditation:

- Concentration Meditation: In this type of meditation, practitioners focus on just one thing, usually their breath, a candle flame, or a mantra. They gently nudge the mind to the selected focal point when it strays.

- Open Monitoring (Vipassana) Meditation: This meditation entails impartially watching ideas, feelings, and bodily sensations as they arise.

- Body Scan Meditation: This is a guided technique where participants mentally examine their bodies, focusing on tight or uncomfortable spots.

- Loving-Kindness (Metta) Meditation:

- Walking meditation: This mindfulness technique takes slow, deliberate walks while being aware of every step and breath.

The psychological and emotional symptoms associated with social anxiety represent another severe subset of symptoms. These symptoms may be severe and incapacitating. Even if they happen in your head, they can do serious harm. The feelings evoked by social encounters can be devastating if you suffer from social anxiety. You may become very self-conscious, imagine only the worst, have very poor self-esteem, and punish yourself for any mistakes you make. This results in a variety of emotional and psychological problems, such as:

- a strong dread of receiving unfavorable feedback, usually because of poor social performance
- A persistent fear of talking or acting in an awkward way
- Extreme discomfort or inferiority complexes when approaching authority figures
- the worry that people with social anxiety will see how uncomfortable they are and reject them as a result.
- An intense reluctance to speak up or strike up a conversation out of fear of being written off as pushy, ignorant, or incompetent

- an excessive (and uneasy) sense of giddiness or joy when receiving compliments or applause from others
- a strong desire to never be in the spotlight

The crippling fear of social events before they emerge is known as anticipatory anxiety.

- Embarrassment and inferiority complexes during real social interactions
- Severe assessments of oneself after speaking with others or engaging in various social situations

All of these symptoms revolve around worries, and these fears are nearly never grounded in an accurate appraisal of the likely course of events. However, the intensity of these anxieties can be so great that you will stop at nothing to prevent circumstances that set off your social anxiety and cause these symptoms.

The behavioral signs of social anxiety are the last group. The psychological and physical symptoms that were previously stated can cause you to form avoidant behaviors, in which you avoid situations that cause you great stress or that you perceive as potentially dangerous. These behaviors can be quite damaging and restricting. Your ability to make new friends, pursue romantic relationships, apply for jobs, follow your interests, go to college, learn from others, participate in sports, volunteer for causes you believe in, and form new relationships will all be impacted if you start to avoid specific social situations. You may avoid particular situations to prevent your social anxiety from worsening, regardless of your other feelings (passion, interest, curiosity, and connection). Such actions could undermine your life's fulfillment and pleasure. The social scenarios that you would want to steer clear of are:

- social events or private get-togethers with strangers
- Communications with high-ranking officials or renowned, accomplished persons
- meeting new individuals in situations where chitchat is expected

- Answering or placing calls
- requesting aid from workers at government agencies, establishments, or passersby
- Interviews for jobs or school
- giving a public speech or performing in front of an audience, such as playing an instrument or sport.
- gatherings of relatives that are more distant
- interactions with former coworkers, classmates, and other acquaintances that you fear could criticize you for not making as much progress in life as you have
- having to wait in line for people who want to talk at banks, retail

establishments, or government institutions

• Dating or any other circumstance that presents the chance for closer social contact

• Online discussion boards or chat rooms where it's normal to get unfavorable comments or insults

Let's now investigate the potential causes of your social anxiety. Genetics is a crucial component. Another element is the anatomy of your brain. The size and functionality of your brain affect your vulnerability to anxiety disorders since different areas of your brain are in charge of different functions. Specifically, the parts of your brain that regulate your fear reactions and the retention and recall of your emotional and phobic memories. Other than that, anxiety symptoms can be exacerbated and contributed to by your personality traits (such as shyness and nervousness from childhood), life history (such as exposure to stressful or negative events), other health conditions (such as thyroid problems, which can increase your risk of anxiety), and use of certain stimulants (like caffeine). An additional perspective on your anxiety is that it is an innate reaction to risk that is ongoing. Humans have always relied on their fear response, often known as their fight-or-flight response. When we were in danger, our sympathetic nervous systems forced our bodies to respond swiftly to maximize our chances of survival. Fear and anxiety developed as a warning sign to trigger that reaction. Even though you're not in a life-threatening circumstance right now, your nervous system nevertheless triggers your fight-or-flight response when it shouldn't. This is the cause of your anxiousness. You only need to teach your body and mind how to refocus your energies if you want to conquer your anxiety. But later, more on conquering anxiety.

Let's now discuss the final point of this chapter, which is the risks associated with unmanaging your anxiety. First of all, depression is frequently the result of untreated anxiety. These two conditions frequently coexist, and they share several symptoms. Both include anxiety, restlessness, sleeplessness, and trouble focusing. Suicide is a potential consequence of this. A significant portion of suicide victims have a diagnosis of a mental health condition. Depression and anxiety are included in this. You must, therefore, take proactive measures to manage your social anxiety to protect your physical and mental safety. Substance misuse is another problem that can be brought on by social anxiety. You run a higher chance of developing an addiction to alcohol, nicotine, and other drugs if you suffer from anxiety disorders. You can start consuming drugs in an attempt to manage your symptoms or elevate your mood. Although there is no proof that alcohol reduces anxiety, a lot of people nevertheless think that it can make them feel happier and more at ease. And while using certain drugs, some people do report feeling a brief improvement in their anxiety. These are not, however, permanent fixes. They will just increase your anxiety and cause dependency as well as other physical and mental problems. Your social anxiety may also lead to the development of certain medical ailments.

These are the risks that social anxiety poses in the near term. The long-term consequences include the onset of heart disease or impeding heart disease recovery. This is

because worry can obstruct several factors. You will begin to live by your anxiousness, which will also throw off your daily routine and timetables. You will put off doing something if you are too nervous. You will stay away from this location completely if you are too nervous to go there. This will impose several restrictions and limitations on your life. And last, anxiety can harm your brain and raise your chance of developing dementia in later life. People's prefrontal cortex and hippocampal structural degradation have been linked to anxiety.

After learning everything there is to know about social anxiety, try going through the symptoms and marking the ones that resonate with you as a quick exercise. What occurs to you when you experience anxiety? To help you reflect on them later, put all of your responses in writing. This will assist you in raising your awareness each time you experience anxiety. The first step in solving an issue is recognizing it. Asking yourself what detrimental consequences social anxiety has had on your life thus far is another quick exercise you can complete. Put your responses in writing. This can support you in taking stock of your life and reinforcing your resolve to get over your worries. In the upcoming chapter, You will discover what can exacerbate your social anxiety.

Origins of Anxiety

Genetic Elements

Anxiety disorders are frequently inherited. Current studies have focused in

on specific genes linked to an increased incidence of anxiety disorders. Some of these genes control the levels of neurotransmitters linked to mood and anxiety, like gamma-aminobutyric acid (GABA) and serotonin. While anxiety disorders can run in families, genetics does not always play a major role in determining a person's risk of developing them. Alternatively, they can significantly increase the danger in the circumstance. In addition to preexisting genetic susceptibility, environmental factors and life experiences play a critical role in the development and manifestation of anxiety. In recent years, there has been a surge in research efforts to identify genetic markers that may indicate vulnerability to anxiety disorders. With this understanding, we might be able to develop more specialized methods of treating anxiety sufferers and reducing the condition's general prevalence.

Neurobiology and Brain Chemistry

New findings in the field of neuroscience have illuminated the

the sophisticated connection between nervous sensations and brain chemistry.

Because of their roles in controlling the stress response and regulating emotions, the amygdala, prefrontal cortex, and hippocampus have drawn much attention from researchers. The current study found that people with anxiety disorders typically had an imbalance in the levels of neurotransmitters that control mood. Among these neurotransmitters are GABA, norepinephrine, and serotonin. A person's body may become more vulnerable to the effects of stress as a result of these changes, which raises the possibility that they may develop anxiety disorders. Beneficial information has also been discovered through research into the endocannabinoidsystem, which controls emotional reactions like stress and anxiety. Drugs or other lifestyle modifications may be used in the future to alter this system in anxiety therapy.

Stress in the Environment

stresses from the environment, especially ones that are experienced often
have been demonstrated to play a significant role in the emergence and maintenance of anxiety disorders throughout time. A few examples of modern people's many pressures are worries about their career and financial status, arguments with friends and family, and the pressure to perform well in school. New research has revealed, for

the first time, how stress appears in the brain and how the body's natural stress response system functions. The hippocampus and the amygdala are the brain regions required for processing memories and emotions. Studies have shown that prolonged stress may disrupt the body's hypothalamic-pituitary-adrenal (HPA) axis, altering the size of these two brain regions. This axis is in charge of controlling the body's stress reaction. A disturbance in the HPA axis can lead to an exaggerated stress response, which might be one of the causes of anxiety disorders, both in their development and persistence. To develop treatments targeted at reducing the negative effects of stress on mental health, a deeper understanding of the relationship between external stressors and the brain's stress response system is necessary. The impact of environmental stressors on anxiety levels can be mitigated with the use of behavioral and psychological therapy.

Childhood Experiences and Trauma

According to recent studies, an individual's early life experiences, particularly traumatic ones have a big role in determining the likelihood that individuals may experience anxiety problems in the future. Abuse, neglect, or witnessing violent behavior as a child may all have long-term effects on the developing brain and stress response of that child. Even in settings where a person feels fairly comfortable, these alterations may increase their likelihood of experiencing anxiety. Epigenetics has also received a lot of attention in recent research. Epigenetic modifications brought on by traumatic experiences influence a person's response to stress and their risk of developing an anxiety disorder.

Comprehending the enduring effects that childhood trauma could have on an individual's mental well-being is essential for both early intervention and trauma-informed therapy. There are hopeful indicators of success with anxiety disorder treatments that address the unique requirements of those who have experienced traumatic events.

Cognitive Patterns and Personality Factors

Current studies have examined the potential role that personality characteristics and Cognitive habits influence anxiety disorders. High levels of neuroticism or negative emotionality, for instance, have been associated in studies with a higher risk of anxiety disorders.

An increased risk of anxiety is generally linked to cognitive activities such as ruminating, worrying, and envisioning the worst possible outcomes. To gain a better understanding of this process, recent research has looked into the role that cognitive biases—such as an attentional bias towards threat-related information—play in the emergence and maintenance of anxiety disorders. Cognitive-behavioral therapies (CBT) are based on studying individual differences and cognitive styles and aim to change maladaptive thought processes. Two cutting-edge CBT techniques that have shown potential in helping patients with anxiety disorders enhance their mental processes and reduce their symptoms are acceptance and commitment therapy (ACT) and mindfulness-based treatments. The two of the

These kinds of treatments are CBT-based.

The Brain-Gut Relationship

The connection between the digestive system and the brain is known as the "gut-brain axis."

System and the brain, thanks to current studies on anxiety disorders, have come under closer examination. It may impact a person's capacity to control emotions and cognitive function. An increasing body of research suggests that anxiety and mood disorders are associated with dysbiosis or an imbalance of the gut microbiota. Serotonin and GABA are two neurotransmitters produced by gut bacteria and are essential for preserving emotional stability. According to recent research, changes in the production of neurotransmitters have been linked to aberrations in the gut flora. Allows signals to travel both ways from the brain to the gastrointestinal system, which may contribute to the emergence of anxiety symptoms. The main objectives of recent studies on probiotics, prebiotics, and nutritional treatments have been to cure anxiety symptoms and modify the gut flora. The discovery of a link between the brain and the stomach has led to the development of cutting-edge complementary and alternative therapies for anxiety.

Further investigation into this field could lead to novel medications that utilize the gut microbiome to treat mental health conditions. Therefore, there is no single factor that causes anxiety disorders; rather, a complex interaction of elements, including genetics, neurology, environment, and psychology, causes them. Recent discoveries in the fields of neuroscience, genetics, and the lifetime effects of trauma have clarified the reasons for anxiety. These findings contribute to the development of more successful and individually tailored prevention and therapeutic approaches, offering a ray of hope to individuals who suffer from anxiety disorders.

Maintaining Mental Clarity and a Clutter-Free Mind Over Time

Long-term habits and lifestyle adjustments are necessary to keep a clutter-free mind:

1. Maintain organization: Regularly examine and clean your physical area, digital files, and obligations.

2. Meditation and mindfulness: These two practices can assist you in developing mental clarity and getting rid of mental clutter.

3. Prioritise Your Tasks: Concentrate on one thing at a time and set a priority list to prevent mental clutter and overwhelm.

4. Set Boundaries: To prevent overcommitting and unnecessary mental

burdens, learn to say no and set boundaries.

5. Writing down your ideas, tasks, and thoughts regularly will help you organize and purify your thoughts.

6. Stay organized: Use calendars and to-do lists, and manage your tasks effectively.

7. Good Lifestyle: To keep a healthy mind that helps reduce mental clutter.

8. Manage Information Overload: Restrict the quantity of information you take in and exercise caution when selecting what to retain in your memory.

9. Practice Gratitude: Clear your mind of tension and unhappy thoughts by

concentrating on what you have instead of what you need.

10. Let Go of the Past: As they might lead to mental clutter, let go of old grudges, errors, and regrets. Acquire knowledge and advance.

Over time, consistency and focus on these techniques will help you clear your mind of clutter.

In summary

, it is about accepting a life free of mental baggage.

Finding calm in a frequently noisy and distracting world can seem impossible. But picture a life where the clutter disappears, making room for harmony and efficiency. This is what a decluttered mind can offer.

Imagine waking up to a clean mental environment free of unnecessary fears and disorganized ideas. Accept the freedom that results from having a clear priority list, laser-like focus, and limitless creativity in your mind. It's a journey towards simplicity, but the rewards are immense.

You're doing more than just clearing your head when you walk along this path of transformation. You are entering a new phase of purpose and clarity. You free your thoughts from the unimportant with every step, creating room for your goals, interests, and relationships—the things that count.

Begin now and witness the powerful effects of a clear mind. Allow the chaos to subside and reveal your infinite potential. Discover yourself and live life to the fullest. This is the potential of a clear mind: an adventure to welcome, an

Section Two

Principal Reasons For Anxiety Disorder

You must first determine the causes and dates of your concern to comprehend it. Consider anxiety like a sickness or a virus. Scientists first look for a virus's original host or carrier when trying to find a cure for that specific sickness. Once the source of the infection has been identified, researchers can move on to comprehend the enemy and develop a vaccine. The same applies to our worry; we must determine the underlying reason behind our feelings.

The majority of people will only state, "I've always had anxiety; there has never been a period when I wasn't anxious." When in reality, you have experienced anxiety-free periods at least occasionally. Some kind of catalyst or trigger always brings on anxiety. Your spouse walking out on you, a family member passing away, seeing a clown, a spider, etc. Simply put, you haven't given it enough attention or actively suppressed the idea. In one way or another, everything began at a specific moment. This problem will be dealt with in this chapter.

This book will cover the theory underlying your anxiety and practical exercises. This will be one of the more hands-on chapters. You must get a pen and paper or use the computer's notepad. Then, make an effort to remember as much as you can. Remember when it was all just beginning? Go back to your earliest memory, the period when you were anxiety-free. Proceed through your recollections until you reach the moment where you recall experiencing panic and worry.

You need to give it much thought once you can pinpoint when your memories become worrisome rather than worry-free. It comes naturally to certain people. They may have a depressing or painful memory from that period. Others may view it as a very little recollection they have never thought about. It could take some time to get through this section, but try to stay with it and record as many thoughts as possible about the moment you start feeling worried.

Once you've jotted down as many memories as you can recall, carefully browse over them to see if anything jumps out at you. Things usually get clearer, and you notice things that you wouldn't ordinarily see once you've put things in writing. Your level of anxiety is usually correlated with a certain situation that you have encountered. The list that follows is what the book's author, Nick, who suffers from both social anxiety and agoraphobia, wrote and came up with when completing this particular exercise.

● My earliest recollection is of playing and having a good time with my pals when I was little.

● A memory from before anxiety strikes: hanging out with pals late into the night when I was a teenager.

● About the moment anxiety strikes - While on vacation, I nearly missed the bathroom stop when riding a bus.

About the time, anxiousness sets in—in a crowded school and on the verge of never using the loo again.

● Uneasy recollections: experiencing panic episodes before starting school and feeling inadequate.

The list illustrates that the memories encountered may be sufficient for an individual to begin feeling anxious. Since each person is unique, your memories may differ greatly from those of another. Some people intensely fear clowns, while others are completely enamored with them. This could result from a frightening experience you experienced as a child. This is a crucial stage in overcoming your anxiety, so when you read through your recollections, make sure everything you write down is true!

This will most likely be your main cause if you come across a specific scenario that you remember and you identify it as a potential anxiety trigger. Your current state of anxiousness is entirely a result of the one or two events you've had. The coach scenario was the first to cause concern for the author, which surfaced when the school situation did. The confluence of circumstances was what set off his anxiousness. It might have been one for you, or it might have been a mix of several. Never discount it until you are positive that you have identified the source of the memory yourself.

It will get emotionally taxing in some places from now on, so keep this in mind:

Things will get difficult and difficult to handle, but imagine living a life free from suffering, hurt, fear, and anxiety.

Now that you've identified the underlying cause, it's time to consider your feelings. Compare your current feelings with how you felt back then. Examine every detail you can recall, then put it all in writing. Writing down your feelings is a great approach to learning more about yourself and having a deeper knowledge of your thoughts.

Taking Care of Your Triggers

It's time to deal with your triggers now that you have determined what may be the underlying source of your anxiety. A trigger is an event, thing, or circumstance that sets off a panic episode. It's similar to throwing a bath bomb into the water—it fizzes and gets out of control when it touches the water. The same is true for anxiety; the trigger for you may differ greatly from that of another person based on the nature of your concern.

Take out your pen and paper once more, and record all the occasions in your life when you have been nervous or experienced a panic attack. This is the list of triggers you will use. Make a note of each panic episode you experience on the list. You ought to eventually have a solid list of circumstances and the exact moment your concern started.

You should have a list of memories you reviewed in the previous chapter and your list of triggers. Now is the time to compare any similarities or differences between your trigger and memory lists. Simply circle the memory if your triggers coincide with or are comparable to that particular memory. After you've reviewed everything and circled a memory. This is unquestionably the main source of your concern.

For once, you know why you're feeling nervous. Understanding your triggers also helps you prevent reliving that experience.

But if your anxiety is unreasonable or beginning to interfere with your day-to-day activities. The easiest way to determine whether your anxiety is problematic is to ask yourself whether it is connected to any problems at all. You may determine whether your anxiety is an issue in several ways. To identify it, start by asking yourself questions.

• Do relationships suffer as a result of this anxiety? It may be problematic if your anxiety is making your relationships difficult since it's a recurring issue that has to be resolved or if it's because you're too insecure to keep up a connection.

• Is my performance at work or school being negatively impacted by my anxiety? It may be an issue if your anxiety starts to affect how well you function at your job or school, making you struggle or perform below expectations in both settings.

Do my nervous thoughts cause me to lose focus on the task? You can be experiencing anxiety symptoms if you believe that your worry is starting to interfere with your ability to complete tasks because you worry too much.

• Is my anxiety preventing me from doing things I used to enjoy? You may have problematic anxiety when your anxiety starts to keep you from participating in activities that you used to like quite a bit or when it makes you unwilling to try a new interest.

- Do I always feel tense and restless, even when there's no good cause? You may have troublesome anxiety if you feel anxious all the time about a bad outcome for which you have no proof or support.

- Even if my impression at the time appears accurate, do I often make things worse than they truly are? Making mountains out of molehills is the term used to describe the tendency to exaggerate situations and may indicate the presence of worry.

Even though you were never aware of it before, you might be nervous if you answered "yes" to any of these questions or gave them some serious thought. To gain a better understanding and determine whether you are, in fact, apprehensive, you can ask a loved one who knows you well to respond to similar questions about yourself. Other individuals could likely see the signs even while you cannot.

To begin with, though, you must learn to control your anxiety when you sense a panic attack coming on. Even though it could be challenging, you will struggle if your initial response to a panic attack is fear of what will happen. Breathe deeply a few times and tell yourself it's all right. This is the time to use any mantras or affirmations you use to help you stay calm. If so, try taking a deep breath before moving on to another relaxing method.

"Heraclitus once said, 'The only constant in life is change."

Why accepting change is crucial to living the life you want

The Greek philosopher Heraclitus, who lived in the sixth century, is quoted in that passage, which still holds today.

Everybody will inevitably experience change. Both minor daily adjustments and significant, life-altering events cause us to undergo both good and negative changes.

You can undoubtedly recall multiple instances of both personal and professional transformation that you have gone through.

It might be a small issue. Perhaps a corporate client needs to reschedule, which gives you more time to close more deals, find new customers, and earn higher commissions.

Alternatively, the modification can have a more profound effect on every aspect of your life. Maybe a family member requires more time since they were suddenly rendered helpless in a terrible auto accident.

We all have to cope with change, whether positive or negative, enjoyable or depressing. The way you handle it will decide how it affects you. How do you overcome it to go on to a better life, or do you use it to enrich yours?

Your chances of personally and professionally succeeding will increase with your ability to embrace change and adjust to changing conditions in life.

There are advantages to accepting change.

It's common for change to surprise you, and it's simple to view it negatively. However, accepting change enables you to recognize its potentially beneficial effects.

Accepting change promotes development in all aspects of your life.

Because it makes us do things we're not comfortable doing, most of us dislike change. It causes us to feel "uncomfortable" and forces us outside our comfort zone.

We must adapt and develop new skills because we are powerless over change. This enables us to develop and showcase talents, abilities, and skills that we always had within of us but weren't aware we had.

Accepting change makes you more flexible and adaptive.

Being at ease allows us to become set in our ways and consistently carry out the same actions because they are convenient or provide us with security and assurance. We become more anxious, vulnerable, and insecure when we cannot adjust to novel circumstances that alter the present.

Accepting change makes us flexible enough to adjust to new circumstances, people, and situations and take advantage of the chances they present. You can find ways to grow and progress when you embrace change with a positive attitude. You might never have found these opportunities if you weren't willing to jump at the chance without hesitation.

Accepting change enables you to reassess and validate your beliefs.

We approach every new event in life with preexisting notions, attitudes, and convictions. This isn't always a negative thing. That is the way things are.

But, you might discover that your perspective changes if you encounter someone who holds entirely different opinions from you or if an event makes you reevaluate some of your deeply held convictions. It might force you to reassess your life or profession, validate preexisting decisions, fortify your convictions, and assist you in reaching even greater heights.

Accepting change reveals your assets.

Your response to life's upheavals reveals your true nature. It reveals qualities in you that you never knew existed or thought you had.

Accepting change allows you to try new things and fail.

It is impossible to grow if you stay in a cozy place and always do the same things. Only through failure can you acquire the most valuable lessons and embark on a successful journey. As we learn to welcome change, we gain more life experiences and understanding of ourselves and others.

Accepting change offers you the bravery to take on more.

You get increasingly skilled at things as you experience more in life. Change is no different. Every time a scenario or environment changes, you are forced to deal with uncertainty or discomfort. And even simpler the next time. It is simpler.

Even though change can be difficult, fear disappears, and the prospect of better possibilities and advancement emerges. Your confidence grows as you consistently accept change, grow more self-assured, and accomplish little objectives. You are, therefore, more likely to follow through and accomplish more ambitious objectives.

Accepting change enables you to deal with failures and recognize accomplishments.

Failures are unavoidable. You will never have perfect circumstances in life. Accepting change allows you to remain optimistic—or at least satisfied—knowing that things will get better despite what may appear to be insurmountable challenges.

The unstated advantage of a setback is that it serves as a reminder of your accomplishments, making your achievement much more pleasant.

Regaining your desired orientation is possible when you accept change.

When you embrace or lean towards change, you take control of your life. You won't always make the correct decision, but doing this will allow you to take the wheel and become an active driver. If needed, you can veer off course or escape.

You can take charge of your life, live your desired life, and stop being a passive bystander.

www.ingramcontent.com/pod-product-compliance
Lightning Source LLC
Chambersburg PA
CBHW052134110526
44591CB00012B/1718